Have You Seen My Umm...Memory?

Coping with Memory Loss

Miller Caldwell

Outskirts Press, Inc.
Denver, Colorado

Dedication

To Jocelyn, my wife.
I apologize for calling you Joan.

To Joan, my sister, who I frequently call Jocelyn.

To Fiona, my first daughter, for calling her Laura
and, of course, to Laura, my second daughter,
for calling her Fiona.

To Bruce, who I regularly forget to call.

To Tache, whose name and bark I will never forget
even although he is now no longer with us.

About the Author

Miller H. Caldwell graduated from London University's School of Oriental and African Studies in 1980, after he had spent five years in Ghana as a fraternal worker and secretary to the Tema Council of Churches. He is the former regional and authority reporter to the Dumfries and Galloway Children's Panels, branch chair of the Scottish Association for the Study of Delinquency, and past president of the Dumfries Burns Club. He is a direct descendant of the poet Robert Burns and a Founding Fellow of the Institute of Contemporary Scotland. Caldwell was diagnosed as suffering from mild cognitive impairment (MCI) in the spring of 2003 and had to retire from the Scottish

Children's Reporter Administration. Released from his onerous responsibilities at work, he marshalled his thoughts and memories constructively and found writing the opportunity and means to improve his memory and health.

Caldwell has published articles in *New Society*, *The Scottish Review*, *The Christian Herald*, and *Good Health Magazine*. He is the honorary Writer in Residence at Dumfries Prison and a member of the Children's Panel Advisory Committee in Dumfries & Galloway.

Other published works by Miller Caldwell include *Operation Oboe*, a historical novel; *Restless Waves*, a travel novel; *7.7 on the Richter Scale*, a diary of life as the camp manager in the North-West Frontier Province of Pakistan after the 2005 earthquake; Ponderings which is a collection of short stories and poems in larger print and *Poet's Progeny*, a selective biography of Robert Burns' descendents. He is currently writing his autobiography, under the title Untied Laces.

He lives in Dumfries, Scotland, with his wife.

For more details of his interesting and varied work and life visit www.millercaldwell.org

Foreword

Have you seen my...umm...memory?

All of us have memory lapses. We justify such occurrences as the consequence of living increasingly busy lives compounded by the gradual aging process. The clinical extremes of Alzheimer's disease and dementia attract justified medical and media attention. Some positive medical news surrounds these ailments and there are optimistic sounds being heard for their case management. But what of the intermediate memory loss phase. The phase that demands early retirement from work, causes family bewilderment, and personal self-doubt? The realization of being in possession of an increasingly suspect memory dawns slowly.

This is not a textbook on mental health, although the author's mild cognitive impairment (MCI) is the background to this book. It is not written in a technical language. It is written for the person in the street because none of us knows what is round the corner in life. For those who have turned that corner and found confusion, memory lapses, and depression, this book is for you, too, because you are not alone. The future is not permanently bleak and there are opportunities to reflect on experiences and to enjoy life more.

I do not talk of "cure" but rather of finding in a multitude of experiences—some bizarre, some funny, some thought-provoking—ways to recapture a quality of life with more pleasure and satisfaction. I gladly share this part of my life in which memory can be brought to heel, laughed at, reviewed, and placed in context. It provides a personal pastiche of the power and the failings of the human memory. A much-needed self-help guide to assist you in managing *your* memory is woven into this book. Accordingly, the mind can relax while the tips are absorbed.

Let Confucius set us on our way:

"I hear and I forget. I see and I remember!"

Contents

Chapter 1

**Sticks and stones may break my bones
But names will never hurt me.**

My empty lunchbox lay on the passenger's seat as I left the picturesque rest stop in rural southwest Scotland. Just then, a thought occurred to me. I could not remember the names of the children I had taken to the Sheriff Court that morning.

I had conducted the case of two children whose parents denied the grounds for referral, and the sheriff had found the cases established. But all of a sudden, I could not remember the names of the children concerned. I turned off the car radio, concentrated hard, but the names just would not come. I drove on

1

to the next rest stop, switched off the car engine, and gave it one last effort. Defeated, I took my case from the back seat and opened it. The names on the files stared at me. How could this have happened? I put it down to overwork. Well, yes… I suppose stress but so what? Were we not all stressed in this frantic new millennium?

The following month, driving back from the supermarket, somehow the road did not seem familiar. I drove on and turned left at the lights hoping to find more familiar territory. I must have driven for a further three minutes before I realized where I was in the town where I had lived in for the past twelve years.

Once more I justified the confusion in my mind. After all, apart from being the head of department, I was the chair of two other organizations and had just been appointed to chair the child protection committee in the area in which I worked.

I made an appointment with my general practitioner who would be bound to see the stress symptoms of my self-diagnosis and give me a period of time to recover on sick leave. The garden would benefit. The dog would have an additional afternoon walk. I could read all the books I had put aside for a wet day and the piano and the oboe would have more regular practice. It was really a question of how long I would be given. Colleagues with similar symptoms had often been given three or four months. Four months would take me to early summer. Perhaps the house would really have a spring clean on time this year. It was time to get things back in order. The unnecessary stigma of stress was diminishing. I was beginning to welcome my self-diagnosis because I knew its medication was simply rest.

In reality, my diagnosis was wide of the mark! My doctor wished me to undergo a series of medical examinations. First came the clinical psychiatrist whose questions seemed so mundane that it was like a social meeting rather than a consultation until he concluded the appointment with a referral to a clinical psychologist and an appointment was also made for a brain scan.

The photographic slices of my brain and its apparent dormant activity were sent to the psychologist and an appointment was made for an hour's testing.

Fifteen unconnected words were recited to me and repeated before I attempted to recall the list. Somehow after considerable concentration, only two words surfaced. I could not remember any more. The list was read out again and this time I focussed on the middle of the list but could only recall four words and neither of the original two that I had got correctly after the first round reappeared. A different list was recited and I fared no better. I was simply unable to recollect these lists despite conducting a two-way conversation ably with the psychologist.

"Count down from ninety-three in sevens, please." Now whose brain at the best of times works like that? I can recite any of the multiplication tables and divide or add, but leave subtraction in multiples of seven to the pocket calculator. I struggled here with the subtraction. Wouldn't you?

"Give me fifteen unrelated words and no proper names, beginning with the letter 'F.'" Oh f—! Why "F"? I momentarily mused at the psychologist's choice of letter. Yet the words fell frequently from a flowing mind. "Failure, fraud, faded, faults, facts, figures, frigidity, fortune, fables, fixtures, fractures, football, furniture, freeze and frost." I felt satisfied that I had not only found enough words but was able to count the right number required. I had used my fingers under the table!

"Umm, some negative thoughts predominating there. Try the same with the letter 'S.'"

I go full steam ahead again making his point redundant. "Sex, satisfaction, success, siblings, savory, sailing, sunshine, snow, silver, sumptuous, seafood, shade, sunbeams, softness, and to finish with, star!" Other tests followed. Which floor was I on in the building? Then a game of placing difficult shapes into a sequenced order. The going got tougher. I found it an increasing challenge.

The conclusion of this appointment resulted in the diagnosis of mild cognitive impairment (MCI), a condition I had never heard of. I had to write it down on a piece of paper. There were apparently two sources of my condition and neither could be adequately isolated.

The first was that I had been prescribed for high

blood pressure medication two years previously and the HBP may have led to a short-term memory default. The other source was confirmed as the consequences of a near-fatal operation some four years ago when, one Sunday evening, I was taken to the hospital suffering an appendix pain. This operation, which is not uncommon in youth, results in surgery that usually leaves a scar of little significance. Unfortunately, by the time the surgeon operated on me that evening, peritonitis had set in and the penetrating surgical knife was met by bacterial infection spread throughout the abdominal cavity. Significant levels of anaesthesia were administered as the operation progressed. The increased amount of anaesthetic undoubtedly saved my life, as the surgeon informed me the next day while inspecting the twenty-two metal staple stitches on my stomach. But the additional anaesthetic may also have caused damage to my short- term memory. Without it, however, I would have died.

The implications for my work were stark. I could not afford to place a child's life at risk if my memory was sufficiently damaged or if I forgot case law or if a child's warrant lapsed due to my failing memory. The psychologist agreed, retirement on ill health grounds was deemed necessary. He would make a further appointment with an occupational physician and assess me every six months to see how my memory was responding.

By the time I had seen the occupational physician, I knew that my professional working life was over. It was nevertheless a valuable meeting at which the arrangements for adaptation to early retirement financially, emotionally, and medically were addressed.

So, at the age of fifty-two, after a working life that had encompassed five years in West Africa as a missionary, four years in Stirling as an educational social worker, and twenty years as a reporter to the children's panels in Kilmarnock, Ayr, and latterly Dumfries, I had retired. I had retired due to a diagnosis of ill health. Retired with MCI. I looked up this medical term on the Internet. I was not familiar with it.

Researchers are attempting to clarify the boundaries between the memory effects of normal aging and the onset of Alzheimer's disease. Cognitive function, abilities such as language, critical thinking, reading and writing, is measured on a continuum between normal and early signs of the disease. This transitional area in the continuum has been labelled mild cognitive impairment—a memory disorder that is a strong early predictor of Alzheimer's disease. It is estimated that there are nearly four million Americans who have Alzheimer's disease. But the number of people who have mild cognitive impairment is still unknown. Studies to determine its prevalence are just beginning. What's more, doctors often use varying criteria when making their diagnosis. Therefore, reliable numbers aren't yet available to determine how common MCI may be.

MCI refers to a specific type of memory loss. People with this disorder have sharp thinking and reasoning skills, but their short-term memory declines. Typically, people with the disorder have the most trouble remembering recently acquired information and knowledge, while their recall of long ago events may remain intact.

The area of the brain responsible for processing storing and recalling new knowledge and information is the hippocampus. You have one at each side of the brain. It is located toward the middle in each of the temporal lobes—portions of your brain that extend from beneath your temples to just behind your ears.

The hippocampus plays a crucial role in your memory system by sorting new information and sending it to other sections of your brain for storage. The hippocampus then recalls information when it's needed. It also connects your new memories with other related memories. Just like my Google searches and entering my favorite links!

So in a nutshell, as it were, my condition of MCI is summed up as being a sharp mind, shaky memory. Useful signposts, but where would this lead me? But first, what really is memory?

Miller Caldwell

<u>What Is Memory?</u>

Memory is all about retaining information and being able to use it. Having a good memory or a poor memory does not necessarily mean that other skills or abilities will be affected likewise.

<u>Different Types of Memory</u>

There are different types of memory skills, not a single memory ability. For example, remembering a name that you have heard for the first time is different from remembering the name of your primary school. Also, remembering how to drive a car is different from recalling an event from your childhood. Memory for skills such as driving a car may often be unaffected in people with everyday memory difficulties. Remembering things that happened many years ago is usually easier than remembering something that happened yesterday, partly because older memories may be especially meaningful and tend to be rehearsed over and over again.

Trying to find the right word while having a conversation, such as remembering what something is called, is also a form of memory difficulty, but one which cannot be easily improved and is not covered in detail here. If you are in such a position—and if it is possible—wait for a moment, since the word may come back to you. Going through letters of the alphabet or thinking of other associations may also help to bring the word to mind.

The advice I offer will mainly be concerned with shorter-term memory difficulties, such as remembering messages, people's names, etc. Longer-term memory difficulties—such as remembering events from many years ago—are less common. If you have such difficulties, you may find that keeping a diary or looking at photographs will help to make such events easier to keep in mind.

<u>Different Stages of Remembering</u>

When we remember something for the first time, there are usually three stages involved. **The learning stage** is what happens when we concentrate on something for the very first time. **The storage stage** occurs when things we've learned are stored in the brain. **The recall stage** is when we try to bring to mind what we've learned. If any of these stages is affected, then a memory lapse may occur. While there is usually little we can do to improve the storage stage of memory, we can usually do something about the learning and recall stages. Much of this book is about offering advice and suggestions as to how you may try to improve your learning and recall skills.

Miller Caldwell

Things to Bear in Mind

Firstly, no one's memory is perfect! We all tend to forget things from time to time. You may find it useful to keep a diary for a few days of your memory lapses—this will help you see that your memory may not in fact be all that bad and it will also help pinpoint those areas of your memory that you need to work on. What stays in our memory will often depend on how keen we are on remembering the matter in question, how interesting it is, etc. As you are now reading this book, you may well find you are now more aware of memory lapses, compared to a few years ago. However, let me stress it is important to realize that your brain was never perfect. You shouldn't say things to yourself such as "My memory is hopeless" or, "I'm stupid, I'm always forgetting things." This may make you feel that your memory is worse than it actually is. If you really are forgetful lots of times, try to keep a sense of humor about it. Coping with memory failures by staying calm and patient, and being open about any memory difficulties, is as important a skill to develop as improving memory in the first place. In fact, these lessons helped to create this entire book!

Secondly, try to be well organized in your everyday routine. This may mean only doing certain things at certain times of the day or on certain days of the week, putting things away or filing things carefully in their own place, not allowing the place where you work or live to get cluttered, etc.

Have You Seen My Umm...Memory?

Thirdly, a poor memory is sometimes the result of poor concentration or trying to do too many things at once. When you are doing one thing, try to concentrate on it and don't let your mind wander on to other things. You will learn best in a setting that is mostly free of distractions. When you find such a place, get into the habit of using it regularly. If you are motivated to remember or learn something, it will help your concentration enormously, so try to think of ways to improve your motivation if something initially appears to be rather boring.

Fourthly, if you are under stress or anxiety then this is likely to have a harmful effect on your memory. You may find that if you are more relaxed about things and make your lifestyle more easy-going, this itself may help improve your memory.

Finally, it is important to remember that being more forgetful is a normal part of growing older; that alcohol and drugs may have a harmful effect on memory; and that you are more likely to be forgetful when you are not feeling well. For example, forgetfulness can occur when you are exhausted after a hard day's work, when you are tired due to poor sleep, when you have headaches or are in any sort of pain.

So we now turn to ways of improving memory. Note that this is not a cure for memory problems. At the moment there are no drugs or treatments that will result in a permanently improved memory. Instead I concentrate on the three main ways in which you can help to improve your memory.

They are:

- Using memory aids
- Learning in better ways
- Recalling in better ways

It is impossible to cover all memory problems but some of the ideas can be adapted to suit different situations. You might even have your own methods that are every bit as valid as the ones that follow.

Have someone slowly read out loud the list of words below. If you don't have anyone handy, read the list to yourself, then close the page. Take three minutes to write down all the words you remember.

Orange	Cloud	Egg	Gate
Chair	River	Apple	Pen
Ball	Hill	Train	Frame
Tree	Book	Shop	Road

End of Chapter TIP:
Try not to do too many things at once.

Chapter 2

**Words are, of course,
the most powerful drug used by mankind.**

Rudyard Kipling

F rancis Bacon declared that "the remedy is worse than the disease." How wrong I have found this to be.

It may have been still winter, often wet and always cold, but it began to be a productive four months in my life. Armed with a shaky memory but a sharp mind I decided to sit down and write a novel!

I had this novel somewhere in my mind. I knew I would rely on my own past experiences in Africa and had been given the encouragement to write a book frequently at parties when my stories came out in a slow, protracted manner. "You should write a book, Miller." I had heard this so often. So that is what I sat down to do.

I kept a list of the characters, their dates of birth, and, well… very little else. I found the book wrote itself! I happily sat at the computer and wrote often eleven hours a day making breaks only for shopping, occasional cooking, and dog walking. After three and a half months I had written 82,500 words. (An average novel is about 75,000 words.) Spell-checked and proofread by my wife, Jocelyn, the general consensus was that I had indeed produced a novel. I had used a few quotations and contacted publishers to obtain their permission to use their authors' quotes. All gave me encouragement and permission except one publisher who requested a £50 fee. That process took a further three months.

Then I discovered from an advertisement in a writer's magazine for Authorsonline.co.uk. At first it was their Wendy who encouraged me to get into print and explained my options. I sent her my manuscript and when her reply came, it was very encouraging. So I ordered some local flyers to announce the arrival of *Operation Oboe*, "a historical novel set in an era when a growing number of women were appointed as diplomats in many parts of the world but were not appointed by the British. Fleur was oblivious to this discrimination and relished the challenge her unusual background gave her. Throughout these decades of conflict and strife an oboe plays unaccompanied. Its notes would linger to entertain an independent Gold Coast." I ordered five thousand flyers and they came in three cardboard boxes.

When the postman came to our door one morning, he dropped three items through the letterbox. The first was a flyer from Tesco Stores, the second was an envelope addressed to "The Occupier" and the third was a distance learning flyer. A thought flew through my head. I could do a post box drop with a flyer. That would keep me active in fresh air and advertise the novel. However, before putting this plan into action I came across a Kleeneze brochure, which invited me to join their distributor pool.

So within a few days I was an up-and-running Kleeneze distributor, offering my supplementary flyer separate to the brochure into letterboxes and occasionally having doorstep conversations. Kleeneze sales increased too with this approach but I was only in this position for three months although I could have continued for as long as I wished. There is never a shortage of distributors. This profitable and enjoyable pastime would suit many with my condition. If it arouses your interest, look out for your next Kleeneze brochure and follow it up by all means. I look back on that escapade with much satisfaction for several reasons. Firstly, it was undertaken over the hottest summer we have had for years. Not a drop of rain fell on me once. Secondly, I had a message for the Kleeneze management. It was my intention to see the Neighbourhood Watch supporter badge shown more prominently. It was at that time on the corner of each brochure. I suggested it should be larger and visible on each distributor's blue satchel. The reason I gave was to show Kleeneze did have a partnership with Neighborhood Watch and that it was a visible sign to give greater confidence to the public who may not welcome each catalogue drop. This initiative was welcomed enthusiastically by the sales director, who wrote to tell me. However, my most humorous delivery took place when I delivered an order for a miniature carpet vacuum cleaner.

The customer was an elderly widow who was delighted to receive her purchase promptly. She invited me into her home to unpack it for her. I appreciated that so much; packaging is a challenge to open these days. So out came the parts and I duly assembled them before her grateful eyes. The instructions popped out and were retrieved by the lady.

"These are no use," she said. "The instructions are in Japanese!"

I turned the instructions over. "Seems like an adequate translation in English on this side," I said. We laughed. However, there could be no demonstration as the transformer required a two-hour charge before use. That did not dampen her enthusiasm. She found another use for my visit.

"Follow me through to the bedroom, please!" she demanded. "I am having a wee problem in bed these days."

I was not sure what she had in mind. I hesitated.

"Come a way in, you'll soon see what's the matter." I entered the bedroom cautiously and saw the source of her distress. Her bed had only three legs! I was able to go under the bed and find the missing fourth leg, attach it to the base, and screw it back into place. I asked her how long it had been like that. She said she had slept on her bedside chair all winter. We really need to get to know our neighbors better.

Research International is a rather grand-sounding organization. It is another ideal opportunity for those with a poor memory wishing to do something useful. I was taken on immediately and welcomed to the Birmingham-based UNEX international postal survey. I had become one of their panelists. It is a project with members taking part in over twenty countries worldwide. They conduct the survey on behalf of their clients, Royal Mail and IPC, and this research provides a continuous monitor of the quality of service of international letters. It measures mail transit times from posting to receipt by customers between the IPC member states in Europe, the USA, and Canada, and from some of the countries to Japan and Brazil. Now that sounds like a full-time job and an interesting and demanding one too.

In reality, all I have to do is post letters each day in a specific post box and record the time of posting. I do so on a sheet of paper, and then transfer the data to their Web site. In my case it involves a dog walk. The chore takes no more than ten minutes each day with gift vouchers delivered every four weeks. They are very useful to use in main town shops. If you wish to enjoy sending letters all over the world and keep to a daily routine, then why not join me as a panelist? Visit either www.research-int.com or unex.research-int.com, or write to Adam Bonehill, UK Agency Manager, Research International at 6&7 Swan Lane Industrial Estate, Birmingham B70 0NU. They would be delighted to hear from you. I have been undertaking this work for over a year now and it is another way to get fresh air, make a contribution to the working life, and discipline my memory to a daily routine.

Responding to a local paper advertisement last summer, I attended the Theatre Royal in Dumfries. It is the oldest-running theater in Scotland and the cast of Red Rose had gathered in a Palm Tree Production to film the life of Robert Burns. The cast included Michael Rodgers, Lucy Russell, Isla Sinclair, and Will Armour. I hesitate to add my own name to the credits but indeed I can. The crew was looking for some extras of all ages and lo and behold after some makeup and a change of attire, I became a French peasant. I had to sit in the stalls of the theater with filled rows in front of me and behind. We were asked to chant in French, reading from a board on stage. The lights were switched off and the cameras filmed from the floor. We learned afterwards that thus we had become a crowd scene in Paris. The revolutionary parapets would be super-imposed at our backs in the cutting room and the fervent French Revolution, for which Robert Burns had some sympathy, was filmed. The chant I had to deliver? I now have no recollection of shouting it but the film was given its première in Dumfries in September 2004 and I was invited to attend.

REMEMBERING PEOPLE'S NAMES

We have new neighbors. Tony built his home near ours and soon we introduced ourselves. Tony remembered my name but I had to be reminded of his. Why? This is a sample of my first conversation with Tony: "Hi Miller. Good to meet you, Miller. We were wondering who our neighbors might be, Miller. We'll have you round for a drink soon, Miller. Oh Miller, bring your wife too. What's her name, Miller?"

Tony is a plumbing and heating engineer. To forget a name may mean losing a customer, so he emphasizes my name until it sticks. Am I offended? Of course not! Most people enjoy hearing their name being spoken. If you doubt this, thank the cashier next time you are in the supermarket by us-ing his or her name displayed on their identity card and see them smile. It's a pity we don't meet the taxman personally!

If there are a number of names you have to re-member, write them in a diary or notebook. Adding what each person does or the person's position—such as the dentist, the dentist's receptionist, or the dentist's hygienist—will also help. Going over the names from time to time will be beneficial, especially if at the same time you try to picture the person's face. Some electronic organizers come with the facility to make pictures of faces that can be stored along with the name. Most digital cameras, some palmtop organizers, and even some watches have the facility to store photographs of faces along with names.

In the case of a foreign-sounding name, you may have to alter the way it sounds to make it more meaningful, e.g. Mustafa can become Must Have A. A long name is best split up into shorter words. In some cases, the name may bring a picture to mind, e.g. Mr. Butcher. But in other cases you may have to twist the name slightly to make it sound more meaningful, e.g. jams for James and cone for Cohen.

If you are trying to remember either the first and second names, or the names of a couple of people, you can form a word, one you can easily picture from the initial letters of the two names. For Harry Thompson, you could form the word and the mind picture word HaT, and imagine Harry wearing a hat. For Mary and Peter, you could make the word MaP and see them both studying a map. One technique that may be difficult to learn, and is therefore not suitable for everyone, is to make an unusual link between a mental image and the person's name. For example, for James Cohen, you could imagine him eating from an ice-cream cone with jam on the top, and so when you meet the person next you would think of jam on an ice-cream cone and then think of the name James (jam) Cohen (cone)! Don't worry about making up an unusual picture—the better the name will stick in your memory. Take one Miller Caldwell. Do you see a Miller at a mill looking down a well to see the cold water? Or do you see a killer mauling a well—he's Killer Maldwell!! Let your imagination run riot! Make your own rules—as long as they work for you.

Another tactic is to consider whether this person has something about their appearance you could associate this with his name. In the case of our Mr. Cohen, if he had a beard you could imagine the beard being the shape of a cone. Remember to concentrate on their face or physical appearance rather than dress or hairstyles that can change overnight.

It may also be helpful to link the person with someone who has the same name and whom you know well, perhaps one of your friends or a famous personality. Try to think of some similarities—for instance, in occupation or appearance—between the person you are meeting for the first time and the other one you already know well. For example, if someone is called Peter Church, you could think of the name Churchill and try to think of some similarity between the person's appearance or occupation and that of Winston Churchill. A taxi driver thus drives Churchill; a smoker offers Churchill a cigar!

When saying good-bye to someone, try to make a habit of saying their name again (e.g. "It was nice meeting you, Fred"). Try to recall their face and name a short while later and try to do this if possible every few hours and over the next few days. If you used any technique for learning to associate the face with the name, try to think of it when you are rehearsing it.

When you find you cannot remember a person's name, try not to panic! Try going through possible names beginning with each letter of the alphabet, if you have time. Think where you learned the name and anything that you may have linked with the name. Don't give up immediately after trying to remember the name; if you try again later, it may come back to you. If, after trying a number of times, you still can't recall the name, don't be afraid to ask the person his or her name. You could say something like this: "I remember you very well, but your name has slipped my mind for the moment." Or you could say your own name as you shake hands with the person. He or she may instinctively do the same when they shake hands with you. Of course, don't ever forget that you can often have a friendly chat with someone without actually saying their name!

REMEMBER WHERE YOU PUT IT

Alarm devices are available than can be attached to a key chain, and which give out a sound and a flashing light when you make a noise, such as whistling or clapping your hands. Although these devices can sometimes be unreliable, they may be useful if you are often losing things such as keys.

One way to make sure that things such as pens are in their right place is to attach a piece of Velcro to the pen and another piece to some other surface. If you get into the habit of always placing the pen against the Velcro pad after you have finished using it, then you are less likely to misplace the pen. You'll also see names taped onto favorite pens in offices. You see professional and clerical staff forget where they put their pens too.

Try to be well organized about where you place things. Spend some time (e.g. a half hour one Saturday morning) making things a little more organized and putting back things that have got out of place. Have set places in your home or office for specific things you use—everyday things like keys, purse, glasses, and mail, money items, etc. Try to get into a habit of putting things away carefully and returning them to their proper place after use. Use labels on cupboards or jars where you tend to keep particular things. For small things you might like to have a plastic, see-through container with its own drawers, such as you find in DIY stores.

It's a good idea to put self-adhesive labels, with a name and telephone number, on certain things such as umbrellas or calendars that you tend to leave lying around. In fact, anything that can be lost or mislaid should have a label on it. For things such as coats, gloves, etc., it is usually possible to buy pens or stamps that can write or print a name and telephone number, or cloth labels that can be sewn into or ironed onto parts of a garment. If you are worried about your home telephone number, you could put your work number or that of someone else who does not mind. If you are out shopping, try to carry things together in a single bag or briefcase. If you are carrying several bags, see if you can put some inside each other—the fewer bags you have to carry, the less likely you are to leave one somewhere. Also, if you sit down and put something like an umbrella or a bag near you, put it in front of you so it can be easily seen; you are then less likely to leave it behind. If you are putting items on the luggage rack of a train, it is a good idea to put them in front on the rack opposite to where you are sitting, so that they are within your view. If you are carrying several things around with you, keep in your mind the number of things you have, and then check from time to time that you still have that number of items.

If, like me, you tend to forget where you have parked your car, try to get into the habit of parking it in a regular place. If you park in a parking lot, try to park it near some part that sticks out such as a tree, a sign, or pay kiosk. When you leave the car, write down the floor level and any other information that will help you find it again. When you are walking away from the car, glance back at it a few times and concentrate on where you have left it.

Have You Seen My Umm...Memory?

Some cars can be fitted with a remote control alarm system; with these systems, pressing the key fob may cause lights to flash or the horn to sound. If you are in the wrong parking lot and there is no response to the remote control, then cancel your signal and move to another parking lot or a different part of the lot. You may be remembering yesterday's parking position! Another tactic involves digital cameras. Digital cameras can record your position from a few yards and when you return to your car, you can delete the picture, ready for the next time.

Be extra vigilant in situations where you are likely to leave things lying around, such as when travelling on busses or trains, when you are given keys, when you use your phone card, etc. You can help a similar sufferer too. If a fellow passenger forgets his or her belongings, don't be afraid to say, "Excuse me, is that your case / umbrella / newspaper?" Not only does that make you feel a worthy citizen, the passenger will appreciate the near loss situation and thank you. Maybe his memory is worse than yours.

If, on the other hand, you have difficulty in finding something which you put away some time earlier, try to go back in your own mind to when you last remembered having the thing. Then go through step by step what you did and where you were after that. You can also pretend that you are putting the thing away again for the first time and think of the likely places you would put it. It is often helpful first of all to look very carefully in the most likely places, and later on look in the less likely places. I am a real culprit here. When I lose something I tell my wife, Jocelyn. She looks for it and finds it. Instead of thanking her promptly I say, "But I've looked there." Oh, no I haven't. I've overlooked there! Apology required.

It can be very frustrating if you cannot find something that you have put away. If you still cannot find it after searching, try to pause, relax for a few minutes or take the dog for a walk, and ask yourself how important the thing really is. After all, it wasn't the holiday flight tickets or a winning lottery ticket, was it? No, most probably not. Can you make do with something else for the time being? Can someone lend you it or is it feasible to buy another one?

Even if you forget to pay for your gas, as I have, don't panic. The police will arrive and understand an honest mistake. Let them know you do have a memory problem as the situation may reoccur. But tape a card on the steering wheel marked "Paid yet?" This will remind you if you start to drive away without paying.

REMEMBER TO DO SOMETHING

It is usually helpful to have prompts, which will help you remind you of things you have to do. For example, if you if you have to take something from home to be repaired or returned, leave it near the front door so that you see it when you leave the house the next morning. Or if you always look in the hall mirror before you go out, stick a note or write a message in lipstick to remind you. Some find that they remember to do something later on if they have an unusual reminder in their view most of the time, such as a watch on the wrong wrist, or a rubber band round a finger. If you wish to do something at lunchtime away from work, put a note in your sandwich box as a timely reminder. If you need to attend to something when you get home after work, then place a Post-It on your bag/handbag or kitchen door.

It is now possible to buy electronic organizers and watches in which you can enter things you have to do. When the alarm goes off, they will also show the message you entered. You can also buy pill-boxes with the days of the week written on them, to help you take tablets regularly. You may be able to have daily or regular pills in a foil pack which is already day marked. Ensure you keep to the correct days to make this system foolproof. Ask your doctor if you can have a dated blister pack if your present medication comes in a bottle.

Some paging companies offer a service whereby they will send a message to a pager on a set date or at regular times. Others prefer to have a white dry-erase board in a prominent place, often the kitchen wall or office wall. The board can be divided into various sections, such as things to buy, people to call, general things to do, or things to do on a set date or at a particular time. Circle in red the most important or urgent messages. Keep a pencil and paper handy at your bedside in case, during the night, you suddenly think of something important that you have to do. If you don't have these at hand, put something such as a watch or pillow in an unusual position near your bed or pull out a bedside drawer, so that when you wake you will realize there is something to remember to do. In the morning, attend to this thing immediately after rising, otherwise you may forget about it in the morning rush.

Keeping a diary, a wall-chart or wall calendar is an obvious help in remembering to do something. If you keep a diary, check it regularly both to write down the things to be done and to cross out the things you have already done. The wall-calendar must be hung somewhere you see every day. Write your list of family anniversaries at the start of the year, and make sure last year's December calendar notes the January anniversaries.

Using Post-It notes, pieces of masking tape, or a little notebook for writing reminders is something that most people find useful. For some things, you could use the back of your checkbook to write on. It is important when you think of something you have to do later on, that you write that thing down immediately in your diary or notebook rather than leaving it to another time. When you write down several things that you have to do, try to arrange them into meaningful groups, or try to find some sort of link between them. If you are going on vacation, write down a list of things that you have to take. If you have a white dry-erase board, you could use this. Tick off the things as you pack them and take a final look at the list when you are about to leave home.

On vacation it is easy to get out of regular home habits. If you need to take medication on vacation, place your pills by your toothbrush in the bathroom or on top of the TV if they are to be taken at night and you the last thing you do before retiring to bed is switch off the television. In general and especially on vacation, try to get into a routine to do things at set times in the day—perhaps with one thing always following on from another—and on set days of the week.

If you have a long list of things to purchase, for example food you buy in a supermarket, and you don't have time to write things down on a piece of paper, try to group them together in some meaningful way. For example, vegetables and fruit could go together; cheese, milk and butter could go together as dairy products, and so on. You could group items according to their size or their color, too. If you have to do something at a particular place, picture the place in your mind and imagine doing the thing in question. For example, if you have to post a letter when you are near a shop, imagine the shop and picture yourself posting the letter when you leave the shop.

Even after a few seconds something may be forgotten. For example, the toast needs to be reheated. Put it in the toaster and repeat the word "toast" slowly, ten times. Hey, presto! Your toast is ready. If you forget this ritual your reminder is likely to be the smoke alarm!

If you lead a very busy life, and who doesn't these days, try to get into the habit of regularly thinking about the things you have to do. This way, you are more likely to keep them in your mind. If you go over such things at set times, for example when you start work in the morning, after lunch, etc., you will more easily keep them in your mind.

People often forget whether or not they have already done a particular thing (such as put a light out, turned off an oven, shut a window, let the cat out, etc.). One way to help in these circumstances is to say aloud what you are doing at the time. "That's the light out!" "That's the oven off!" "That's the window shut!" or "That's the cat out!"

TIP:
Keep to a fixed routine, with set things
at set times of the day

Chapter 3

"I forgot," Lennie said softly. "I tried not to forget. Honest to God I did, George."

John Steinbeck, *Of Mice and Men*

Managing *Your Memory* (ISBN 0 9517930 04) is a manual produced for improving everyday memory skills. It was written by Dr. Narinder Kapur of the Wessex Neurological Centre, Southampton General Hospital. I was delighted to receive this booklet reminding me that memory lapses affect us all, old and young, able-bodied and disabled. It is also a booklet for those who think they have no memory lapses, helping to prevent memory lapses in the first place as well as giving guidance for those trying to cope better with memory difficulties when they do occur. When I contacted the author by e-mail indicating I wished to refer to his booklet, I added that I would have to save the message I was sending as I was bound to forget I had written to him unless I had a record of the message. I gave him my address but in common with many MCI sufferers, I neither have a mobile phone nor a desire to communicate by telephone. Recalling messages is one of the most difficult tasks. "Write it down," I hear you say. Well, if I do that I loose the conversation. Honestly, I know what I'm talking about. Please don't ring me! Write or e-mail me but please...not the phone!

Professor Kapur was delighted to hear I was writing this book and gave me permission to add his manual to the text of this book. You can obtain a copy of his booklet from the Secretary of the Wessex Neurological Centre, Southampton General Hospital, Southampton SO16 6YD, England.

At school some forty years ago we had an annual competition. It was a general knowledge test paper with increasingly difficult questions to answer. That meant that the whole school, every class, took this one test. On no fewer than three occasions I came in at the top of my class and received a prize at the end of the term. I still have these books embossed with the school badge and its motto, Serva Fidem (keep faith). One way to assess my memory after I left work was to engage in quizzes. I began viewing *Countdown* on Channel 4 but found the math difficult in the time given and I had no ability to regularly have more than a five-letter word ready in thirty seconds. Indeed, too many four-letter words were more common! Prior to this program was *Fifteen-to-One*, a quiz that whittled down fifteen competitors to a finalist within a half-hour program. I began to watch and answer these questions for fun and to challenge my memory. After viewing this program for a few weeks, I felt confident to take up their offer at the close of the program and I decided to apply.

I found their application form online and filled it in. I attached a photograph as requested and posted the envelope. Six weeks later I received an invitation to attend an audition in Glasgow at the Mitchell Library.

When I got there I was surprised to find ninety people present. That meant six rounds of Fifteen-to-One and I sat through five of them to listen to their performances. I spoke to several contemporary contenders. To my surprise many felt quizzes improved their memories and that is why they liked the discipline of facing the cameras to challenge themselves. I was not alone. We were certainly not seeking fame or fortune.

Eventually I was called up and stood in an arc of fifteen contenders. I probably got 75 percent of my questions correct but perhaps my accent or my age or my town of domesticity were the deciding factors for me to receive a letter indicating I was on the short list and would appear later in the series. I had much sympathy for one of the Glasgow contestants. He stood in his white Arab robes and faced particularly challenging questions. One question, which made me cringe and feel for him, was: "Which wine of France is associated with the town of Beaune?" Failing to answer that question, he was asked, "What did Sir Walter Raleigh bring to Britain in the seventeenth century?" It seemed so inappropriate for a Muslim to be answering questions on wine and tobacco. I was not, however, called to the present series and, to date, the program has not been on air.

Nevertheless, this experience encouraged me to enter into another, if similar, adventure. I was invited to Carlisle to have an audition for *The Weakest Link*. We assembled in the foyer of the Crown and Mitre hotel pending our auditions on the second floor. There were nine of us: two young manicured glamorous girls, a single father who had brought along his six-year-old son, one man from Kelso in the Borders, a female primary-school teacher, a man from Newcastle, a barmaid from Cumbria, and a single mother from Westmoreland. Their motives were worn on their sleeves. The young glamorous girls were looking for that televized opportunity to change their lives. The single father was bright and ready to show how well he was coping as a single parent. He presented well and was a credit for Justice for Fathers. The Geordie had taken early retirement recently and decided to follow a singing career. Any exposure would benefit his cause and it did not take him long to arrange a gig at the Cumbrian barmaid's work setting.

All of us were meant to bring to the audition any unusual abilities or experiences. I had given this some thought on my application. Due to work in West Africa in the '70s, I have retained a conversational standard of speaking Akan Twi so that was recorded under the "languages" heading. As the past president of the Dumfries Burns Club, I also offered to recite some Burns if required but the pièce de résistance was concealed in my back pocket. It was my Xaphoon. I had come across this unusual but very easy-to-play instrument in a youth hostel magazine. For a little change short of £40 I had purchased one by post three months earlier. It advertised itself as the Pocket Sax. It consists of a hollow fingerboard with a tenor saxophone reed attached to the end. It makes a remarkably loud sound—especially in the bath—and although pitched in the key of C, it lends itself to play best in the keys of D, F, G, Gm, Dm, and Am. It is akin to a clarinet in tone or a miniature saxophone.

Playing the Xaphoon, the guitar, piano, or drums is particularly good for those whose memories are unreliable. When you change gears while driving a car, make a cup of tea, or tie your shoelaces, you are on autopilot. This is also true after music practice. Your fingers or lips automatically fall into place and your well-practiced piece of music comes to the fore. I had no hesitation in declaring I played the Xaphoon or could recite a Burns' poem. I knew they were deeply ingrained in my memory and would be instantly recalled on demand. Nevertheless, I taped the word "Auld" onto the reed. That would remind me that the program, which was to be broadcast on Jan. 25—Burns Night—would have Auld Lang Syne played on the Xaphoon at Anne Robinson's request!

We were led into a hotel conference room in which an arc of chairs had been placed before a table. We were asked to write our names on a sticky label and place it prominently on our person. Thereafter we were given a minute to answer twenty general knowledge questions. So far so good. A mock *Weakest Link* game then followed in which I managed not only to "bank" on an empty bank but when selecting the weakest link on my board I wrote "Nicola." According to the producer, I was the first contestant ever to have selected as my weakest link, a name that was not the name of a contestant! I wondered how this happened but was given some encouragement by the single father, who said he saw my problem. "Nicola" wore her label on her jacket but it was partly covered by her lapel. From my position, I thought I could see Nic, so I wrote "Nicola." When Michelle realized that I was referring to her as Nicola, she was dumbfounded. Indeed her name was Michelle but she had an identical twin and her name was Nicola! I could only declare I must have been psychic!

Each of us then had an individual interview in front of a camera. I was asked to recite Burns and

gave a careful rendering of "To a Mouse." I got to
the second verse before being cut...

> *...I'm truly sorry man's dominion*
> *Has broken Nature's social union*
> *An justifies that ill opinion,*
> *Which makes thee startle*
> *At me, they poor, earth-born companion,*
> *An' fellow mortal!*

The Xaphoon continued the Burns theme with a
rendering of "A Man's a Man For a' That." As I
suspected this small instrument filled the room with
a loud mellow tone and surprised the producers,
who demanded an encore. Flushed by these performances, I rounded off the individual interview
with a smattering of the Akan Twi language. At the
end of the audition I was asked by one of the competitors if I needed a lift. Although I was only a
stone's throw away from the station and I had a return ticket, it did get us talking. We confided to
each other that we had both entered for the fun of
it—and to exercise our failing memory.

So I flew to London and arrived at the Pine-
wood studios in the summer to record an edition of
The Weakest Link to be shown the following spring.
The company of the much-feared Anne Robinson
was simply delightful until she took her place on the
podium. I'll forgive her. I had to take three shirts
with me to ensure a suitable coordination with other
competitors was achieved. I was more surprised to

find, however, that I had a hairdresser assigned to me despite being bald. And of course I found the experience rewarding as well as challenging. I am not permitted to record in print what took place or I would be in breach of contract to the BBC. However, the quiz did stimulate my mind and I got off to a fair start, but a confusing question left me cold and I "passed." Having done so, I was the obvious contestant to make the walk of shame. No shame, however; it was good to challenge a weak memory in this way. I have no regrets.

Am I still entering regular quizzes? Well, not at present. Instead I try to complete crosswords in my daily paper. There are questions there that rouse answers automatically. Then there are the answers that have to be teased out from the hidden depths of memory. Thinking links go into overdrive but if I do not complete the crossword, it appears on the table after the evening meal when my wife adds the finishing touches.

After a career of asking pertinent questions of witnesses in courts, it's time to answer more than ask. I suppose that set me off on this path of quizzes. That has meant travel to Glasgow, Carlisle and London. So the tip at this point is:

TIP:
When travelling about, check regularly that you
have everything with you.

REMEMBER WHAT IS SAID

For keeping a daily record of events that have happened, interactions with people, etc., it may be useful to keep a diary that you check over on a regular basis. This is especially important if you lead a busy lifestyle where you have to keep track of where you are in a particular relationship with a particular person. A diary could also be used for more immediate needs, such as remembering messages, especially if it is part of a filofax system where there are separate pages for writing down messages. Again, masking tape can be written on and it peels off easily. The dry-erase board, positioned in a prominent location, provides a handy place for noting what was said at a meeting.

A pocket cassette recorder or electronic organizer is handy for keeping messages too. Tape recorders are available with digital formats enabling you to mark various points along the recording. You can then have different files on the same tape. It is even possible to buy miniature recorders that store short messages, usually around thirty seconds long, and are part of a pen, watch, or small device that can be attached to a key ring.

Try to think about what you hear. Ask yourself questions such as whether you agree or disagree with it. In general, the more you think about something when you first hear or read it, the better it will stick in your memory.

When you have to remember numbers, try to

join them into a group (e.g., remember 3-7-4 not as three-seven-four but as "three hundred and seventy four"). In the case of a long telephone number you may find it useful to split the number into two parts. For example, you could try to remember a number such as 193852 as "one hundred and ninety-three" and "eight hundred and fifty-two." Or you could think of it as the year before the beginning of World War II (1938), together with the number of weeks in the year (52). Similarly, 430 could be remembered as teatime (4:30 p.m.). Grouping numbers together like this or finding meaning in them makes them less likely to be forgotten, especially if you reorganize the numbers in a way that is meaningful to you. This strategy applies equally to other situations, such as remembering strings of letters or letters and numbers.

In the case of a list of things, a useful technique is to form a word from the first letter of the items. For example, if you had to remember to buy bread, eggs, dates, and soap, you could remember that the letters B and D look and sound similar and that E comes after D. Alternatively, you could form a link word out of the first letters of the items. In this example, the link word could be BEDS. Then, by simply going through the letters of the link word you could recall each of the things. It might also be useful to actually associate the link word with the place you are going to, so that you don't forget what you learned the keyword for. In this example, you could make a picture in your mind of some beds in front of the entrance to the supermarket you were going to.

Another similar idea is to form links between the words in a list. So if you had to remember to buy bread, eggs, dates, and soap, you could imagine yourself making an egg and date sandwich and washing your hands with soap before eating it. Of course, good as this is as an exercise to condition your memory, nothing beats a shopping list in print. Cereal packets in our house are always cut up and used as cardboard to write lists on.

If you have forgotten a particular message that has been given to you, try to think about other things to do with the message. Who gave it to you? Where was it given? What were you doing at the time? Were there any similar messages you received at the time? And so on. You may find that this helps to bring back the message to your mind.

Chapter 4

When I was young I could remember anything…whether it happened or not.

Mark Twain

I t is deemed that a child under the age of eight in Scotland could not be a reliable witness in court. However, many exceptions were made to that rule. I have fond memories of the case of a house fire incident I once had to bring to a Children's Hearing. A five-year-old boy was in the care of his grandmother when she succumbed to the effects of excessive alcohol after lighting the cooking pan. The boy failed to arouse his grandmother when the pan caught fire but he did not panic. He telephoned for the fire brigade. Impressed by his actions at the

Children's Hearing, the chairman was surprised the boy knew the number to contact his local fire station. Just to confirm in his mind that the child could remember it, he asked him to repeat it. The boy looked at the chairman in surprise.

"Everybody knows," he said, "…it's 999."

Memories can be revealed in some other unusual ways by young children. I refer to the sad cases of two children who had been sexually abused within their homes. I took the cases to the Sheriff Court at Ayr after their parents denied the alleged abuse. Although I had cited the children to give evidence, I did not expect either to be forthcoming with their evidence. I had relied on other older sibling witnesses but had to be fair to the defense team in citing such young children in case they could shed light on the case. The four-year-old boy and his seven-year-old sister not only proved me wrong, they gave remarkable testimonies.

After the sheriff had put the four-year-old at ease within the court, it was my turn to question him. I had taken along a cardboard box of toys in case the children became restless amid legal debate. But when I began questioning the young lad, he took hold of the box and pushed it around the courtroom as if it was a car he was driving. I followed him at a distance until he stopped by the dock. He took hold of a doll from the box and began hitting it against the wooden panel of the dock. As he struck the doll he recited "Bad man, bad man, bad man." I seized the moment. "Who's a bad man?"

"Uncle Peter," he replied.

"Why is Uncle Peter a bad man?"

The child placed his hand over his genital area and pulled his trousers back and forward. He looked down and said audibly, "He does this to me. Don't like it."

The court was stunned. No cross-examination was forthcoming.

His sister was a delightful chatty girl who told the court of her friends, her school, and her favorite TV programs but when questioned about her abuse, she froze. She could not speak. Such explicit words and actions could not be spoken nor be expected to be said by a child so young. But she could draw. Paper was provided and with the aid of colored crayons and large sheets of white paper, she drew her answers and identified the offenders and what they had done to her and her brother. Sadly such experiences will remain with them for a very long time. Both children had to be removed from their parental home.

Each Children's Hearing in Scotland depends on sensitive and caring members of the public to form three panel members to decide on the best interest of each child before them. One panel member lived on the island of Arran but regularly took cases on the Ayrshire mainland. Her cases were carefully arranged taking account of the two-hour sailing of the ferry between Brodick and Ardrossan. At the end of one hearing in Kilwinning, the reporter was asked to take the panel member to Ardrossan pier as there was still time to catch the 4:30 p.m. sailing home to Arran. The reporter left the papers in the care of the chairman pending his return and set off with Mary. As they approached the port, they could see the ferry was preparing to leave the pier. Time was of the essence. Mary ran from the car and saw to her horror that the ferry was already some eight feet away from the pier. Fortunately there was a member of the crew standing at the exposed railing and she decided to jump into his arms. She took a running leap into mid air as the seaman was shouting at Mary to stop. Nevertheless Mary successfully leapt over the deep water and grabbed the sailor's out-stretched arms. She had made it on board by the skin of her teeth. She would soon be home.

"Ya bloody fool Mary," he said, "We're running late. We've not tied up in Ardrossan yet!"

I went to primary school at the age of four and three quarters. (Additional fractions are very important in the early years.) In first grade we had a spelling book, which I imagine was a universal first spelling book. In the first few pages there were three- and four-letter words, escalating to some very long and unusually spelled words towards the middle and the end of the book. I found the spelling challenging on the first page. When asked to spell the words in the first grouping I failed at the simple word "egg." Of course I knew what an egg was and I had heard it mentioned frequently and eaten it more regularly, but spelling it did not make sense to me. I knew it was a three-letter word. It had to be, to make it audible, I reckoned. But as I weighed up the two possibilities, I could not see the logic in having a double "gg." How do you pronounce "gg"? You can't! So I told the teacher "egg" was spelt this way: EEG. That made sense to me. Now why am I telling you this?

At this early age I realized perception did not always equate with reality. It was such a profound discovery that I can recall the classroom scene as if it was yesterday. Awakened to the reality of life's shades and inconsistencies, is it really necessary always to have a view? Can that view be a temporary vacuum? Yes. Can it be a memory lapse? Most certainly.

REMEMBERING HOW TO GET SOMEWHERE

Having the directions on a clear map is obviously important. Make sure you go over this before you go out, and plan any long journey in stages. Landmarks such as hospitals are usually indicated on road maps, and you may find it useful to make a note of these. Some people prefer an actual map of the route, others prefer the directions written on a piece of paper; choose the one you are happiest with and keep it.

You can now buy navigational aids that are portable or can be fixed in a car. They tell you where you are on a map, how to get to a destination, etc. Car accessory stores and high-tech catalogues usually stock such aids.

Find out if there is a road sign which you can follow to a particular place; it is usually easier to do this than following directions to turn right and left several times. Before you set out, it is also wise to take along with you the telephone number of the destination to which you are heading, and a cell phone if you have one, in case you have to ring someone for further directions.

Some people have difficulty finding their way around a large building. If you have this sort of difficulty, try putting some sticky paper (such as colored shapes and arrows) on the floor or on the wall, with the names of the important places written on the markers. You may also wish to put labels or pictures on the doors of some of the rooms to indicate what they are used for. Now, at first reading you can't see yourself doing any of these things but in large outpatient departments and general hospitals passing staff will understand exactly what you are doing.

If the directions you have to follow are quite long, try to split them up into shorter directions and concentrate on one direction at a time. If someone has told you the directions, repeat back what the person has said to make sure you got it right, and also if possible at intervals after that. Make a mental picture of going in the particular direction you were given. Ask the person if there is a sign to a particular town that is in the same direction as your destination, as this will be easier to follow than a set of turnings. If you are going somewhere on foot, look back a few times at various landmarks so that when you are returning you will be able to recognize places more easily. If you are going by car, you could do the same by looking in your mirror a few times.

If you are trying to learn your way around a new town, try to compare the layout of the streets to somewhere you are familiar with, such as a place you previously lived in for a long time. Take a note of the immediate street names and make a simple spider plan on paper marking the prominent places you come across, e.g. post office, bank, police station, school, or market. Fold this paper and keep it in your pocket, wallet, or purse. When you meet a neighbor you could ask to be given a tour around the district stating that you are not confident to go alone just yet. This is likely to provide you with shortcuts. Without overdoing it, don't forget to repeat your new neighbor's name so you don't have to keep asking him/her for it too often. If you get lost or have difficulty in following some directions, stay calm and don't panic—just try to work through the directions you have already followed and try to think about the other ways you could go. If you have been to your destination before, spend a few minutes thinking back to the directions you followed then. Finally, don't be afraid to ask someone for directions. A gas station is as good as a policeman, and they might ring up the place you are heading for too.

TIP:
Don't forget young children's birthdays. Mark their birthdays in a calendar, and with a marker pen place an asterisk on the previous week to remind you a birthday is looming. That should ensure adequate shopping and posting time is achieved.

Chapter 5

"Happiness is good health and a poor memory."

Ingrid Bergman

ATM cards are becoming necessary these days and of course that gives us potentially more problems. Telephone numbers (landline and mobile), digital locks, fax numbers—they all seem to conspire to defeat us. I admit to being one of relatively few men in their fifties who have no mobile telephone. Online ordering often makes mobile numbers a compulsory field to fill in, and that is where I part company with them.

I recently acquired my new Visa PIN number to accompany the security chip. I produced the card to pay for goods at the local supermarket.

"It's my first time. I'm pleased I remembered the number," I told the young cashier.

"That's fine," he said, "and you don't need to sign now!"

"Just as well. I've forgotten my name anyway!"

He laughed, as did the next customer. Of course, I hadn't forgotten my name but could have forgotten the number quite easily.

Fortunately I was able to change the number to one I could remember and did so the day I received it. Now my chip number is the same as the pin number of my other bankcard. Why give myself additional numbers to remember? And that number? Well yes, I have it written down in my diary despite bank advice not to do so. Not as the number of my bank and chip card, of course. It appears on a page that states a $33.85 refund from Halfords. Needless to say I changed the figures on this occasion, but if you have to write it down, you can easily disguise it this way. Better still, add a few extra entries to foil a thief, e.g. 17:55 return from Euston; Flight number BA3227; Tony's birthday, Nov. 17; Stanley and Sheila's anniversary, July 23. Put them all in your diary. Put the real number first or last. You will remember which is the real number.

This story revolves around the co-operative store in Kirriemuir where I went to do a signing of my novel. Lady Lyle is a sprightly woman in her early nineties. She is a war widow of a famous Victoria Cross holder and lives with her son. He reminded

her recently that her dementia not only placed herself at risk but other road users too. It was time she
handed him her keys of her hatchback. Lady Lyle
accepted that this was a proper decision. Two days
later, however, she had no recollection of this conversation with her son and she set off to go to Kirriemuir to shop. She could not find her car keys. She
resolved this difficulty by finding her son's car keys
and so proceeded to the co-operative shop in his
Rolls Royce! How Ingrid Bergman would have enjoyed that story.

During my work in West Africa, I had the privi-
lege and pleasure of having several cook stewards
working for me over the years. The first was Christian Ahiabu, a native of the Ewe tribe in Ghana.
During his first week, I met my match twice. Firstly
he asked me how I liked my lobster!

Not having been a regular lobster eater in my
youth, I turned the question to him. "How do you
like to serve lobster, Christian?"

"Perhaps I will grill a little cheese on its stomach. The Italians like to eat it that way."

I recalled his CV. He had worked for French,
Italian, British, and American families over the
years. He had amassed great culinary knowledge
and skill. I was the beneficiary of such expertise.

"Well if that's how the Italians like it, Christian,
that's good enough for me!"

Then he arrived back at the house one Saturday
afternoon with a live chicken. Its legs were tied to-

gether with a piece of cloth. Christian opened the kitchen drawer and took out the bread knife. I asked him what he was going to do.

"I have to kill the chicken before you can eat it," he said, smiling and teasing me.

"Yes, of course, but in Scotland the farmer would ring its neck and not use the bread knife."

"Ah," said Christian, "then show me!"

Suddenly I thought of becoming a vegetarian! Nevertheless I was being challenged and if I could teach Christian how to do this, I would have no worries slicing bread again with the bread knife.

I took the chicken under my left arm and held it firmly. It looked at me as if it had found a new friend. But I was past the point of no return. I grabbed the bird's neck, released it from the security of my left arm, and sharply swung the bird round. Once, twice, three times it circled in a fatal twist. I returned the bird to my arms. It shook its feathered neck, looked at me in disgust, and started to chuckle. So did Christian.

"You see," he said with a broad smile, "an African chicken is a tougher bird than your Scottish chicken." I was defeated. I gave the bird over to Christian and in a swift move, the bread knife separated head from body and the meal was prepared.

Christian was an excellent chef. After Christian went on to further his career in Tema harbor, Janet Mensah arrived. I was not going to compare her with Christian and wanted to be fair to her but I soon realized I had a problem. I gave her a shopping list of some nineteen items. She did not take the list. She asked me to read it to her. I read the list clearly and slowly and she gazed at me as if in a drunken stupor. Off she went to the local market and returned a couple of hours later. She unpacked the goods onto the kitchen table.

"Sorry, there was no plain flour in the market today."

Every other item was present. I smiled. Janet had just demonstrated her ability to remember all that was on my list and explained what was missing. It was a most remarkable memory she possessed. Of course, being illiterate forced her to make greater use of her memory yet each shopping list scenario was most impressive. That taught me to make better use of my memory by testing it more often.

One evening in Tema I was asked to chair an inter-church youth quiz. That seemed like an evening of fun but it nearly caused a further disruption of the churches on account of one alert memory!

After four rounds of questions we came to the last round with a game in which I would call out ten Bible texts. The teams of two members—representing the Catholic, Methodist, Presbyterian, Evangelical Presbyterian, AME Zion, Salvation Army, and Lutheran church youth groups—sat poised with their Bibles. Once a team found the text, they were to stand up and read the it out aloud. First to do so gained the point. All was going well. When I called out Psalm 32:1, there was a rush of pages as fingers searched diligently and quiet reassuring calls of "old" came from the teams referring to the Old Testament. A Presbyterian youth member stood up and read: "Happy are those whose sins are forgiven, whose wrongs are pardoned." With that point gained we came to the last question of the round and of the evening. I reminded the teams that it was presently a tie between the Methodist and Catholic youth teams and that I would be watching carefully to see which team stood up first to call out the text. Not a plague of crawling cockroaches would have disturbed the tense atmosphere. I took a drink from a glass of water to extend the excitement further. "Are you ready?" "Yes, yes," they said. "So onward to the final question. The gospel according to… St. John, chapter six… verse—thirty-five."

The question had hardly left my lips when a Methodist team member stood up and confidently said, "I am the Bread of Life, Jesus told them. He who comes to me will never be hungry; he who believes in me will never be thirsty."

"Well done, Methodists. You have won this evening." Then an almighty row erupted. At first I was unable to see where any objection could possibly come from but then it was stated plainly to me by the Catholic team member who seemed to have the support of other teams. The Methodists sat quietly on tender hooks. I had to adjudicate whether the winning point stood. It was being alleged that the winning point was not valid as the answer came without the team looking up the text in the Bible!

Have You Seen My Umm...Memory?

I ruled that what was not in doubt, was that the Methodist team had provided the correct answer. All agreed, so far so good. It then lay on the point as to whether the purpose of the quiz was to train fingers to find texts in the Bible or for the teams to know their Bible. After all, I suspected if any other player had recognized the text straight away in previous rounds, they too would have announced it without looking it up. They reluctantly agreed. In that light I declared that the Methodist team had won. Future quizzes would prove less divisive.

In my cottage on the Greenwich Meridian in Tema, Ghana, I met my wife in 1974. Our relationship nearly got off to a very unfortunate start. I had returned for a second tour of duty to find a letter awaiting me. It was from Jennifer, a Scottish teacher in Bekwai near Kumasi in the center of Ghana. She had received a letter from her friend in Inverness who had met me while I was on home leave, giving an illustrated talk about Ghana. When I learned that this girl in Inverness had a friend in Ghana, it was natural to offer to meet her on my return to Africa, if she was ever in Tema. This letter was the result of that encounter.

Jennifer was a math teacher and she had organized with Jocelyn, the chemistry teacher, a party of twenty pupils to Tema to see some of the town's industrial factories. They would be staying at the Tema Secondary School and wondered if I would be at home to visit on Wednesday evening. That gave me twenty-four hours notice.

When they arrived, love struck me immediately. I was bowled off my feet. But this was a casual meeting of two teachers, Jennifer and Jocelyn and I had only cups of a chocolate drink called Milo and some plain Pioneer biscuits to offer. They had a deadline to return to their pupils, so as I drove them back to the school at 9:30 p.m. so I suggested that they should come for a meal the next night, the last before they travelled north to Bekwai in the Ashanti region.

When I returned home I went into the garden and approached the cage of my African gray parrot, Kofi. He enjoyed his neck being rubbed and true to his mimicking reputation, he responded to the names of Jocelyn and Jennifer after I told him whom I had just met. Then in a most devious manner I decided to concentrate on adding specifically Jocelyn to his vocabulary.

"I love Jocelyn, I love Jocelyn," I chanted. Kofi cocked his head. He would be able to welcome Jocelyn the following evening with this greeting and she would realize I had taught him this and my motive would be clear. The stakes were high.

"I love Jennifer! I love Jennifer!" Somehow this parrot—which not only mimicked perfectly the World Service theme tune, Lilly Bulero, but was able to produce all six BBC pips—was quite unable to get his mind or his beak around the word "Jocelyn." Only "Jennifer" came out.

The following evening Jennifer and Jocelyn arrived and the table was set for a meal. During our meal with the glass louvers wide open to catch the evening breeze, Kofi sat happily on his spar outside shrieking, "I love Jennifer." Inside, Jennifer was most impressed. My scheme had backfired! However, not all was lost and our correspondence started. Despite this inauspicious start, Jocelyn became my wife in January 1977.

In retrospect birds have played their part in our family's misfortune on more than this occasion.

When I was a schoolboy I kept a number of caged birds. I had a cage of zebra finches, waxbills and cordon bleu finches. My interest began with a budgerigar following my father making a pastoral visit to a parishioner. He had set out at 4:30 p.m. but he did not return till after 6:30 p.m. He explained on his return that as he was leaving her home, Mrs. Matheson's budgerigar, which was a prolific talker, squeaked, "What about a cup o' tea then?"

"Oh Mr. Caldwell! I forgot. Let me put the kettle on!" Thereafter tea and cakes were served while Joey the budgie entertained extravagantly.

"I'm not a wee sparrow
I'm not a wee crow
I'm only a wee Budgie
I want ye to know.
Joey Matheson
238 Kilmarnock Road
Glasgow S.3

Who's a clever boy then?"

59

When semi-retirement took my father from Glasgow to rural Perthshire, I was still in West Africa. My caged birds were still alive and had been cared for by my parents during my absence. They too would have to be transported but certainly not in the moving truck. So on a very hot sunny day in June 1974, wearing his clerical collar, my father set off by car from Glasgow to Abernethy. He was concerned that the caged water bottle container was leaking water on the journey and the birds would be thirsty in such heat. As he drove further north his anxiety increased. He decided to park at the Fourways Restaurant at Dunblane where he had enjoyed breaks on previous journeys. He entered the restaurant and caught a waitress's eye.

"Excuse me. I have five birds in the car and I wonder if you could give me some water to take to them."

"Certainly sir, just a moment."

She tried to hide a smirk. It was clear what was going on in the waitress's mind. It was surely a case for the tabloid papers. A few moments later she approached the car with a tray on which she had five long glasses of water each with a straw, ice, and a slice of lemon—for the birds!

That leads me to suggest that while pets are a great comfort and source of unconditional love, the parrot family cannot be relied on to improve memories. Alcohol has a similar effect.

I recall an elderly couple from Glasgow who decided one warm summer evening to set off for

Largs on the Ayrshire coast for a breath of sea air. They failed to lock their car, probably thinking that they would not be staying out long. They enjoyed their walk to the Viking Pencil monument and soon made their way to their vehicle. As they approached their car, they noticed a man was asleep on the back seat!

They opened the door cautiously to find him sound asleep but very well dressed. He even had a flower in the lapel of his jacket. Rather than involve the police, the husband inquired where he lived so that he could drive him home. This led to the drunk man stirring.

"Ma address? Four eight five Glenifer View, Paisley," he managed to say.

"Then that's just fine. We're on our way back to Glasgow so we'll drop you off at your home in Paisley."

The car set off from Largs, through Wemyss Bay, Gourock, Greenock, and Port Glasgow. They drove along the banks of the Clyde and after almost an hour, they entered Paisley. They stopped a "Paisley Buddy" who gave them directions. When they found the tenement building and stopped outside his home, the drunk was still fast asleep. The driver ventured up all four floors of the apartment block until he found the correct door. There was a party going on inside. He knocked harder and harder until the door was opened.

"Come away in, the party's in full swing."

"Excuse me. I wonder if you can give me a

61

hand. I've got your son in the car. He's had a bit too much to drink. Can you help me to bring him up?"

"Naw, Naw. Ye havena got ma son in yer car. Ye see we're havin' a wee party. Ma son wis married this afternoon. He's away on his honeymoon, to Largs."

TIP:
Too much drink spoils the memory.

Chapter 6

"Knowledge comes but wisdom lingers."

Tennyson

tudying and Memorizing for Exams

General Hints:

- Read this section a few times during the term and   especially when you are preparing for an exam.

- Be well organized in TWO areas: your time and the place where you do most of your studying (usually your room).

63

Miller Caldwell

Your Time

Have your routine well planned so that you can study at set times. Try to have a set time for your coursework and a set time for your revision. Try to study in the same place and at the same time so that doing coursework and revision becomes a natural habit. Do not revise when you are tired or upset. In general, earlier in the day is better for revising rather than late in the evening or at night. Although you may find yourself occasionally revising late into the night, make that the exception rather than the rule. We all need sleep! Have set times for re-laxing and for pastimes such as listening to music, watching TV, playing sports, etc. Don't worry how much you think your friends are revising, do what you feel is right for you. If you have been revising regularly over the past few months, then you shouldn't have to cram too much just before the exam. Remember exams aren't everything!

Try to plan how you spend each evening during term time and also how you spend weekends and mid-term breaks. You may find it helpful at the start of each evening to do a detailed time plan for the amount of time that you spend on a piece of coursework or revision. Again, small yellow Post-It notes are useful. You can use them to write down specific times for starting and ending particular top-ics. The more systematic you are when you are planning your work, the easier it will be to get things done.

Don't put off your revision until exam time—do it regularly throughout the year (little and often). If possible try to do some revision each evening and a little every weekend. You could have your revision planned so that you revise different subjects on different days of the week. During any term breaks you may wish to have special revision plans that allow for the extra time you will have then, especially if exams are coming up. You may wish to plan your revision over several weeks and months so that each subject gets a fair share.

It's a good idea to have a calendar on your bedroom wall, preferably one that allows space for notes below each date. If you put your revision program on the calendar, you can see it at a glance. You may prefer to use a diary or even an electronic or computer-based organizer, rather than a calendar. Choose the one that you are most comfortable with.

Your Room

A tidy, well-organized room can help to improve your studying. Try to keep your study desk fairly clear. Have things in set places and put labels on drawers and other places where things are kept. Always put back things in their right places. Having a whiteboard that you can write on may help too. You can use this to write down important things that you have to remember such as a chemical formula or foreign language words.

Good concentration is one of the keys to good studying. Remember to study in a quiet place. If on occasions your home has too many distractions, go somewhere quiet to revise—for example, a library. The more similar the place where you revise is to the place where you will be taking your exams, the more likely that you will be able to recall things on that day.

If you are feeling upset or down about something, this will affect your study concentration. If there are things on your mind, try to deal with these matters first before you start studying. You may find it helpful to talk to an older person about anything that is upsetting you. When you study, try to be in a calm and relaxed state of mind. Try not to concentrate on past failures or unpleasant things that might happen in the future; think of the happy side of things. Saying positive and relaxed things to yourself will help put you in a better state of mind. Remember, things may appear to be upsetting at the time, but later—after a few days or weeks—they may not seem to be all that bad.

There are three basic things to keep in mind when you are trying to remember material that you are reading (or a lecture you are attending), and these can be summarized in the word CAR, which stands for **C**oncentrate, **A**ssociate, and **R**ehearse. Essentially, you need to be sure that you are concentrating and attending well when you are reading the material or listening to the lecture. You can help to do this by firstly asking yourself a question about the topic, keeping this in mind while you are reading or listening, and see how well it is being answered. You need to try to associate what you are reading or hearing with what you already know about the topic or related topics and also try to make links within the material itself. After you have read the material or attended the lecture, you need to rehearse what you have learned—the best way is to test yourself at regular intervals. We will go into more detail on these techniques in the paragraphs below.

- Before you read something for the first time, or before you attend a lecture about something new to you, it is useful to have skimmed through a summary or abstract of what you are about to learn. Having this summary in your mind in advance helps your brain to absorb what you will be reading or hearing in full.

- When you are hearing or reading something for the first time, asking yourself questions about it will help you to pay closer attention. Try to find something meaningful in what you are reading or hearing by linking it to something that you already know well. You may be able to relate what you are studying to some previous work that you have done, or to something you have personally experienced. That way it will stick better in your mind.

- In general, pictures are easier to remember than words. If you can find a picture or even draw a picture that explains what it is you are reading or hearing for the first time, then the information will stick in your mind better than if you just have words alone.

- If you are not sure about something in a lecture, don't be afraid to ask. Know how to find all the things you need for the subject you are studying. Know which people to turn to for help (family, friends, neighbors, lecturers, etc.); where the best libraries are; which books are best; which bits of software or video material may be useful; and whether the Internet may have some useful information. When you get stuck, remember to go through the list of possible ways that could be of help.

- Read at a speed you are comfortable with. It is more important to understand what you read than to whiz through quickly without understanding it. Try to be interested in what you are studying. If you find your work rather boring, try to think of some things that will help to motivate you.

- When you make notes from a lecture or from a book, try to put things down in your own words rather than using the exact words the other person has used. Try to note key points rather than everything the person has said. You can make your own shorthand by using symbols or by using abbreviations of words. Once you have made notes, especially if you used abbreviations during the lecture, go over them again soon afterwards, filling in parts with your ordinary handwriting to make the notes clearer. After you have started to learn a topic for the first time, it is useful to read around it from various angles. Different books could say different things, so try to read several different books that describe the same topic.

- If you have read something that is very long, try to make short notes that describe the content. These could be in the form of "revision cards"; i.e., short notes on ruled index cards. You can have headings for the different parts of your notes and you can have sub-headings as well, such as 1(a), 1(b), 2(a), 2(b). If you give each section a title, then what you are reading may make more sense and may stick better in your mind. If you learn the headings by themselves (like a skeleton), then during the exam you can use these headings to help you remember what to write.

- When you go over a topic, it is useful to space apart any revision rather than to cram all your reading about it into one session. Spacing apart your revision of a topic actually helps it stick better in your memory more than doing all the revision in one session.

- After you have done a long or difficult revision session, or after you have done well in a piece of coursework, give yourself a well-earned break. You deserve it!

Use Mnemonics

- You can use "memory tricks" to help you remember. These memory tricks are called mnemonics—pronounced nem-on-iks. A memory trick for learning a new word could be to think of some other word that is a similar to the new one—and then try to make a connection between the two words. You can use a memory trick to learn foreign words. For example, if you are learning that the French word "glacé" means ice cream, think of eating ice cream out of a glass!

- You can also use memory tricks when you are learning words in science. For example, the optic nerve connects the back of the eye to the brain. Optic sounds like optician.

Have You Seen My Umm...Memory?

- Memory tricks can also help you to remember lists of things. For example, "many people watch fat frogs carrying vitamins" is a memory trick for remembering the parts of living substances: minerals, proteins, water, fat, fiber, carbohydrates, and vitamins. It helps if you can make some link between the list of terms and the sentence that is created as a memory trick, in this case the word "vitamins." As the **P**art **Y**ield **O**f **3** my **B**lood **P**ressure **V**aries. I say this to myself regularly and remember my car registration number accordingly is at present **PY O3 BPV**. Make your phrase to suit your registration. Remember the more distinct you make it, the better it will be to remember.

- Sometimes it may be difficult to think of any memory trick. If you do think of one, make sure it is meaningful to YOU. If it sounds unusual or funny, all the better!

- When you are doing a test or going over revision in your mind, remember to think about any memory tricks that you used.

- Test yourself regularly for the things that you learn. Recalling things again and again, especially from memory and with increasing intervals in between, will help them stick more easily in your mind as opposed to simply reading and re-reading something.

- After you have read something, cover it up and try to recall it. Go back over it again. Which parts did you not get? Concentrate on these the next time. You may find it helpful to underline those parts or highlight them with a highlighter pen.

- When you test yourself or go over things in your mind, remember to go over any headings or mnemonics that you made. Also, try to think about the material you are rehearsing, making links to related topics if possible, asking questions about the material, etc., as this will greatly increase the value of your rehearsal.

- Remember to give yourself tests a few days, weeks, and months after you learned the subject, and not only a few minutes or hours afterwards. Then you will really know how much has stuck in your mind. Highlight or make a note of those important items you did not recall, and spend a little extra time on learning these again, perhaps making links with the items you did recall.

- You can also test yourself in your spare time—for example, when sitting in a car on a long journey. You could use that time to go over things like French verbs, or go over something you've been learning in the past few weeks. Oh, and don't forget to turn off the car stereo system while you recall!

- It is often said that the best way to learn is by teaching. If you can get an opportunity to explain a topic to someone else, perhaps someone in the same course, do so.

- Answering mock exam questions under exam conditions is useful. You could also test yourself on questions you yourself have thought up.

- The day before an exam, it may be useful to go over notes or headings or memory tricks rather than books, e.g. revision cards that you have used in your revision.

Think Carefully in Exams

- Make sure you get a good night's sleep before. Have all things that you will need for the exam sorted out before you go to bed. Treat yourself to a warm bath. Make yourself feel good.

- In the exam itself, read the questions carefully. Underline the key words in the question. Plan your answers, even if this takes a few minutes.

- Make a rough outline of your answers, with headings. Work out roughly how much time you will spend on each part of an answer and always allow some time at the very end so that you can check your answers.

- Put your watch at the front of your desk so that you can be sure you are not spending too much time on any one part of the answer. Check the time every twenty to thirty minutes or so.

- If one question in the exam is very difficult, leave it until after you have finished some of the other questions and then go back to it again.

- If you can't find a word you are thinking of, going through the letters of the alphabet may help.

- When you are thinking of possible answers and nothing comes to mind, try to think of any notes that you made or memory tricks that you used, or think of something similar—the answer may then pop into your head. You may also find it useful to think back to the time and the place when you re-

Have You Seen My Umm...Memory?

vised the topic that is in the exam question.

- After you have done well in an exam, even if you did not come in the top three, give yourself a reward. You deserve it.

Chapter 7

"One touch of nature
makes the whole world kin."

William Shakespeare,
Troilus and Cressida

Here "touch of nature" refers to a short memory. It is common to all mankind.

Nature's healing powers have been studied since time began. How young were we when we learned that a docken leaf would soothe the nettle sting? Why does Granny prefer camomile tea? Why are we catching up on our French cousins and consuming more garlic and red wine these days?

At the age of twenty-three I lay dying. I had

succumbed to a severe bout of malaria despite taking a daily malaprim pill. I was single and exhausted. I had no energy and certainly none to get out of bed go to the local clinic. Dear old Mrs. Swanikier realized how ill I was. She forced me to sit up and drink water but even that was too difficult.

"You must drink," she said with concern on her furrowed brow.

"I will make a tomato soup and you must drink it." I fell back into a dream and moments later she returned with a red consommé, which had more hot pepper in it than I could ever contemplate. Mrs. Swaniker forced this hot soup between my lips and the liquid burned my lips and mouth, roasted my throat, and dissolved into my stomach—but remarkably I was able to take several mouthfuls. The soup was so incredibly peppery hot. A green berry much stronger than a hot chilli had been crushed and mixed in the soup. Mrs. Swaniker knew it would do the trick. Indeed it did. I felt sweat seep from my skin everywhere. As I became wet, strength returned to my body. I began to see clearly again and was able to rise, the first time for several days.

I took a shower and returned to a dry bed. I slept soundly for several hours and when I woke, the parasites had left me and I was on the road to recovery.

Since returning from West Africa we have had a supply of hot pepper power supplied to us over the years. Whenever a cold is starting or a stiffness creeps into the bones, the powder is sprinkled over

our food, the sweat glands erupt, we sweat pro-
fusely—especially my head—and then we feel
much better.

In Ghana I saw grazed knees of children being
soothed by the inner skin of the pawpaw fruit. Far
better than our creams and bandages, these soft
melon-like fruits produce a cool, moist skin that is
always gratefully received by the fallen child.

To celebrate our silver wedding anniversary we
returned to Ghana in 2002 to visit old friends, see
new places, and enjoy the country that brought us
together. One excursion we made was to the Kakum
Canopy Walk in the National Park. From the treetop
canopy walkway a brilliant red flash of wings
makes you focus on a Verreaux's Touraco as it
lands a few feet away on a Kuntan tree. You could
never see this from the forest floor. To get there we
were taken by a conservation guide who was a
qualified botanist. As we proceeded through the
dense vegetation the guide helped us to identify
animal prints in the dried mud. He explained how
distinct marks on a tree resulted from an elephant
scratching his back or how the juicy contents missing from a fruit casing were a monkey's breakfast.

However, I was equally amazed by the botanical
trail, which uncovered plant species used in tradi-
tional medicine. These plants serve to fight infec-
tions, heal wounds, increase lactation, ease muscle
strain, relieve stomach ailments, and eliminate fe-
vers. The guide picked up a chewing sponge con-
taining medicinal properties and explained how it is

still used by the Akan people as a toothbrush. The large unusual Kuntan tree with its roots some fifteen feet above ground is not just unusual in appearance but its leaves are used as natural healing bandages.

These experiences have made me less suspicious of non–National Health Service prescriptions and so when I was prescribed ginkgo, ginseng, red wine, and aspirin daily by my consultant, I thought it time to ascertain why. Could they assist my fading memory?

But just a moment; it is worth recalling how life used to be for me. How I loved a free cold third of a pint of school milk. The concentrated orange juice in square shouldered bottles was simply delicious. Then there was the acquired taste of thick brown malt extract. Perhaps the worst bit was the spoonful of cod liver oil. Yuk! Do you remember how the oil used to drip down the sides of the old glass bottle congealing as it approached the base and sticking to the work surface? It smelled pretty bad too.

In hindsight however, the government and our parents were absolutely right! Our diets and our intellectual development were both improved by these early dietary supplements. Perhaps it is a pity our government does not give them out free to our children today instead of complaining about obesity in childhood and doing little about it.

In those days it was generally recognized that vitamins did you good. Now we know better. Research shows that it's a substance called Omega-3 found in fish oils that is so vital for the health of our brains, hearts, circulation, and joints. Cod liver oil and the omega-3 it contains is possibly the most important supplement that all of us should be taking every day.

Research suggests that ginseng and ginkgo biloba may act together to produce an increase in mental performance and short-term memory. Recently controlled trials using a combination of ginkgo biloba and ginseng demonstrated significant increases in mental performance over a fourteen-week period among healthy volunteers. While previous research has documented the effects of ginkgo on memory, this study is the first using a standardized ginkgo biloba and ginseng extract in combination. This takes us one step beyond the gingko debate.

Keep your general practitioner informed if you are taking herbal medication. There is still a need for greater cooperation between herbal and medical practitioners and how their practices interact.

NB: If you are pregnant, breast feeding, or taking prescription medicines, consult your doctor or pharmacist before using ginkgo biloba.

Miller Caldwell

<u>The Gingko Debate</u>

The Case in Favor

Several studies have concluded that gingko does have some effect, but many studies were flawed. In one of the better studies, people with Alzheimer's disease or similar dementia diseases were given 120mg gingko each day for a year, or a dummy tablet. Those given the gingko did not deteriorate as quickly as those on the dummy tablet. (*Archives of Neurology*, November 1998. *Journal of the American Medical Association*, 1997; p278; 1327-32)

The Case Against

In a Dutch trial, elderly patients with memory impairment were given either gingko or a dummy pill for twenty-four weeks. There was no difference between the two groups in a large number of memory tests. This was a good trial because the researchers used a very convincing dummy tablet with the same taste and smell as real gingko. (*Journal of the American Geriatric Society*, 2000; 48-1-12.)

So gingko biloba and ginseng are what I was advised to take twice daily. I would not continue to take them if I felt they were not beneficial. However, this amelioration may be considerably assisted by the glass of red wine each evening or the dispersible aspirin tablets (BP 75mg), which both thin the blood and aid the corpuscles in the brain to function and flow smoothly. A daily, prolonged-release Cabren Felodipine tablet completes my daily prescription. This is required to keep my blood pressure in check.

Bog myrtle was recommended to us prior to a week's summer holiday in the mosquito-infested countryside of northwest Scotland. It was recommended to us to avoid been bitten each night especially as we were to be near a fresh loch. However, on researching the bog myrtle plant on the Internet, I discovered it is also recommended as a short-term memory helper. One Web site stated: "The leaves, chewed raw or used as a standard infusion, is used as a general tonic and restorative, of special value during bouts of sickness, depression, or strain. It quickly revives the spirit, *quickens the mind* and strengthens the nerves. Cases of poor memory and mental confusion in old age are successfully treated with Bog Myrtle." Garlic cloves and Marmite on toast are equally effective in making the mosquito think you are a vegetable, and hence seek his blood elsewhere!

Warning: The essential bog myrtle oil, reportedly toxic, inhibits growth of various bacteria. Do not use without medical supervision.

In the fifties Dr. Ken Kay was our family doctor in Kirriemuir. One day an elderly lady came to see him as she was not feeling well. Her symptoms were not severe and so to examine her condition more carefully, the doctor asked her to bring a sample of her water the next time she was in town. She arrived back a few days later and handed the good doctor a clear glass bottle with a most dark brown opaque colored liquid inside.

Somewhat alarmed by its color and density, the doctor inquired: "Is your water normally this color?"

"No doctor," came the reply, "just when the burn is in spate!"

My retirement present was a twenty-one-gear bicycle. After I had cycled for three weeks I returned to the cycle shop for an initial service as advised. I asked for a stand to be attached. I was asked if I felt this would be necessary.

"Oh yes, most definitely," I said, "after all, it's not just me who's too tired!"

I am further tempted to tell of the patient whose doctor inquired after a similar cause of premature retirement as mine whether his patient now woke up grumpy these mornings. He replied that it was not necessary; she got up herself!

Joking apart, I trust you do have as much support from family and friends as I do. If not, let your doctor put you in touch with support groups.

Nietzsche commented: "The advantage of a bad

memory is one can enjoy several times the same good things as if it were the first time." If that's your experience, enjoy these family videos again and again!

TIP:
Be systematic; have a place for everything.

Chapter 8

"Memory, the warder of the brain."

Shakespeare, *Macbeth*

MEMORY AIDS

Here is a list of memory aids, some of which you may find helpful in your particular daily routine. Some of them have already been referred to in earlier pages. If you can try out a memory aid for a while, before spending a lot of time and money on it, then all the better. Remember that some of the memory aids described here may not be available where you live. Also note that some electronic memory aids may be replaced or discontinued after a while.

Miller Caldwell

Stationery Memory Aids

<u>Post-It Notes.</u> They come in different colors and sizes and some are pre-printed with message headings. They can be used as a reminder to do things, or as a temporary message pad.

<u>Masking Tape.</u> Since most types of masking tape can be written on, they can in fact be used in the same way as Post-It Notes. Masking tape comes in different widths and can be cut in different lengths. It will stick securely to most types of surfaces and can usually be easily removed without causing any damage.

<u>Notebooks, Diaries, and Filofaxes.</u> Put these in a prominent place where they can be easily and regularly seen. Anything you write should be in CAPITAL letters and in black ink so that it stands out. Different makes of A3-size notelets that can be stuck to most surfaces, including fridge doors.

It is easy to misplace things by leaving them around, but if something has a label stuck on it with a name and telephone number, it is more likely to be returned to the owner. Labels can be easily printed on a computer although some stationery shops will provide such a service. It is also possible to buy pens or stamps that can write or print a name and telephone number onto a garment or umbrella and labels can be sewn on to clothes. If you worry about leaving your own name and telephone number, you could give that of a friend or just give your work telephone number. In some countries, key clubs exist with whom you can register your keys—a number on the key ring will then alert the finder to contact the key club. Some banks offer this service too.

Mechanical Memory Aids

Mechanical Timers. These are inexpensive and very easy to use.

Pill Boxes. Various forms and sizes are available from most chemist shops or pharmacy stores.

Clocks. It may be worth considering mechanical and electronic clocks that have large clear dials or numbers and that also show the day, the month, and the date.

Electronic Storage Aids

Telephone Recording Devices. If you often forget parts of important telephone conversations, there are devices that can be attached to a phone that can record a conversation. Remember that you usually need to tell the person on the other end of the line that you are recording the conversation. The devices are available in a number of high-tech shopping catalogues.

<u>Tape Recorders.</u> These now come in various shapes and sizes. The newer "solid-state" recording devices do not use tape and they allow for easy indexing and searching for items on the recorder. Thus it is possible to have separate files for messages relating to the home, items relating to work, etc.

<u>Digital Cameras.</u> Gone are the days when you needed rolls of film and had to take them to be printed. Now you can snap and delete pictures if unwanted. You will find digital cameras able to record where you parked the car at the football match or shopping mall. A high-resolution copy can be transferred to your computer screen too. Ensure you delete past sites. The photo is only valid during each parking occasion. That's the beauty of the delete button.

Electronic Alarm Aids

<u>Watch Alarms.</u> – Some watch alarms—such as those made by Casio—can store up to five daily message alarms. Thus an alarm can go off in the morning and the word "tablet" can be made to appear at the same time; another alarm can be set off in the evening and so on.

Have You Seen My Umm...Memory?

<u>Power-Timers.</u> These can be set to turn electrical equipment on and off at certain times of the day in case you forget.

<u>Key Finders.</u> If you keep forgetting where you put your keys, a key ring that has an alarm can be bought through a number of shopping catalogues and at car accessory shops. When a loud clapping noise is made the key ring gives off a bleep and a light flashes.

<u>Other Alarms.</u> There are devices, available from catalogues for the partially sighted, which can tell you when a fridge door is left open. There are also some that give an alarm when water in a bathtub goes above a certain level.

Electronic Storage-Alarm Aids

<u>Electronic Organizers.</u> These can be used as diaries, name and address books, and message-alarm devices. Some are now available with pen input onto a screen, rather than pressing keys on a keyboard, and some voice organizers have storage and alarm features but with voice input and output.

<u>Watches.</u> Some watches have the facility to store names and telephone numbers. There are also some that can store short, spoken messages and some then can take and store photographs.

Miller Caldwell

Fixed Communication Aids

Telephones. Most telephones have memory stores, such that you can phone a stored number by pressing a single button. Choose those phones that also have a number display feature so you can see the number you are entering in. "Photophones" are available in some shopping catalogues; with these, a number can be programmed to match a photo of a friend, relative, or a place such as your local hospital. When the photograph is pressed, the number will automatically be dialled. The "amplify" button may also be of benefit to you.

Mobile Communication Aids

Telephones. Many mobile phones now also have the features of electronic organizers, so that items can be stored and message alarms can be programmed. Mobile phones are developing at such a rate, you may prefer to take your needs to the outlets where staff can assist you to make the most appropriate mobile telephone purchase.

Pagers. These can be used to help you remember to do things, as long as you have someone to send the message. Some pagers have built-in alarm functions, such that an alarm can be set to go off every day. Some paging companies offer a Web-based service in which they will send a message to your pager to remind you to do things; for example, take your medicine or attend an appointment.

Navigational Aids. In addition to standard road maps, you can now buy electronic navigation maps that are portable or can be fixed in a car. They tell you where you currently are on a map, the best route to get to a destination, etc. Car accessory stores and high-tech catalogues usually stock such aids.

TIP:
Have a weekly clean-up, not just an annual spring clean. Clutter clogs the mind and the home.

Chapter 9
FREQUENTLY ASKED QUESTIONS

Everybody forgets things from time to time. Those who say they don't must have forgotten! Below are some of the common questions that people ask when their memory has a nap.

Q. How can I remember where I have put my reading glasses?

- Attach a chain or cord to your glasses and wear them around your neck.

- Wear a shirt with a pocket and put your glasses case in the pocket. Stick a name and address label on the glasses in the event of them being mislaid.

- Before going to bed, get into the habit of putting your glasses in the same place.

- Keep a spare pair somewhere else, perhaps in the car.

Q. How can I ensure I don't misplace letters or important documents?

- Have a good, clearly labelled filing system.

- If you do remove documents or letters from a file, make sure   that you put them back in the right place.

Q. How can I remember to take my tablets and check to ensure I have taken them?

- Use a watch with a multi-function alarm that will go off to remind you to take tablets, together with a specially designed pillbox that allows you to see at a glance whether you have taken your medicine.

- Try to link taking your tablets with something that you already do at the same time, such as having a meal or cleaning your teeth.

- Repeat prescriptions can be made by telephone at most surgeries. With three tablets left, it's time to re-order.

Q. How can I remember to take my door key with me when I leave the house?

- Stick a picture of a key on the front door to remind you as you leave.

- Write "KEY" on a piece of masking tape and stick it on the door.

- Keep your door key with something that you know you will be taking with you, such as your purse, wallet, or car keys.

Q. How can I remember to watch a TV program at a particular time or to listen to a particular radio program?

- Keep a dry-erase board next to the TV. Divide it up into the days of the week and with a note of the programs you want to watch or listen to each day.

- On the day of the program, put a Post-It note on the TV or radio.

Q. How can I remember a message that I have been given?

- Write it down somewhere.

- Repeat the message as soon as you have been given it to make sure that you have all the information. Repeat it again several times, leaving longer intervals in between.

- Think about the message and try to make associations between the different parts of it.

Q. I don't enjoy reading anymore because I keep forgetting the plot. How can I improve this?

- There is no easy answer to this question and it may be better to avoid reading lengthy novels.

- You may find you can still enjoy shorter books, ones with illustrations, or books you once read in your childhood.

- If you like poetry, this may be easier to read than a novel.

Q. My partner has severe memory loss. How can I stop him from asking the same question over and over again?

- Put the answer to the question in a prominent place, such as a dry-erase board mounted on a wall. Next time the question is asked, smile and point to the board.

- If your partner keeps on asking the day of the week, buy a watch or clock that displays the day, and encourage him to use this.

Q. What simple steps can I take now?

- Keep your mind active. Memory is like a muscle. Keep it in shape. Consider a hobby that uses your brain—reading, card games, crosswords, or evening classes. Then try to recall the event as vividly as possible. Consider a pet and its needs and its disadvantages. Walk, with or without a dog; play golf weekly; or pick up badminton. These activities lead to social contact. More social contact with other people can lessen the likelihood of serious memory problems.

- Don't smoke. Simply do not smoke. Yes, I know a bit of nicotine can improve brain function very temporarily, but hang on: smoking is likely to damage brain blood vessels and make your problem worse in the long term.

- Get enough sleep. When you sleep, your brain processes the information that you have learned during the day. If you deprive yourself of sleep, the memories won't stick properly. Students who spend the night cramming for exams may be wasting their time. Sleep is like the darkroom of the film developer. Open it prematurely and you lose the picture. Enjoy your sleep. It's good for you.

TIP:
Listen to the answers. Have the answer repeated if necessary. Don't be afraid to tell the speaker that he or she speaks too quickly or too quietly for you.

Chapter 10
FINAL THOUGHTS

Extinctus amabitur idem
How quickly we forget.

Much of the advice of the last few chapters is self-explanatory. You may be using many of these solutions already. You may be using other means not mentioned to get round your memory problems. In any case, what suits you best is what is welcomed.

Remember all of us have lapses from time to time and you don't have to own up to them on every occasion. As we all have had an experience of memory loss and can identify with each sufferer, we quickly forget the matter that has been causing frustration. Being economical with the truth became an expedient way to avoid political embarrassment in recent years and so a precedent was set. There are times when we need not own up to the method we are using. I give you the following example.

Thirty-three years ago I was sent by Camp America to a boys' holiday camp in Massachusetts. There was an American student there who played a twelve-stringed guitar and had a beautiful singing voice. He wrote his own songs. I had often wondered what became of him. Then this summer I heard from one of his colleagues who now works as a consultant psychologist in Vermont. He had found my e-mail address under Operation Oboe in a Google search. I asked him if he ever heard from Dave Hort. He replied that he was now a professional singer and at his Web site I could listen to his music. He told me his musical name was now David Benrexi. I looked him up under that name and found how to contact him and listened to forty of his recorded songs. (www.MyDaddyLovesMe.org). We began to correspond. Then I asked how his brother Gary was doing. He was thrilled to know I had remembered his brother's name, especially as he was not at the campsite at Camp Onota all those years ago. What he did not know was that I had written down the words of one of his compositions in 1972 and have been playing this song from time to time.

Have You Seen My Umm...Memory?

In the early seventies David, like so many others of his age, was waiting to hear if he had drawn a high or low draft number which would determine whether he was going to war in Vietnam. It made that generation of camp counsellors keen to cast off youthfulness prematurely and become fighters or exiles. He wrote a song in that context called "I Don't Want to be Your Shadow Anymore." The chorus, below, is followed by the first verse.

I don't want to be your shadow anymore
I just want to stand in the light for a while;
I won't wait around, looking for your frown
When a smile would better suit my style.

'Twas my brother Gary, told me life is a bitch
And there ain't no sense in being poor, just to spite
*   the rich;*
If you never can be satisfied, tell me why even
*   bother*
Be yourself don't hide your face
Behind the dead dreams of your father.

So it was in his song that I had remembered his brother's name, although thirty-three years had passed and I had never met Gary.

In taking you along my own path to resolve memory problems I must stress that I am not medically trained. That does not prevent me from commenting, as the report from the British Journal of

General Practice states, "there is a general lack of communication between doctors and patients about herbal remedies. Current software used by GPs to compile patient records does not include a facility to record data on alternative medications." It is estimated that at least twelve million Britons regularly use herbal remedies.

My own gingko biloba and ginseng combination and aspirin regimen were prescribed by my psychiatrist. My general practitioner was initially unaware of this prescription. I urge you to consult your general practitioner before you start on any course of herbal treatment in conjunction with any prescribed medication. We owe it to our medical advisers to inform them just what we are taking.

I conclude this short book with a tale. No, not an elephant tale just yet. Instead let me tell you of the experience of a good friend Stuart and his wife Joyce, who were returning home last winter through the beautiful rural countryside of southwest Scotland to their home at dusk when suddenly their car hit a young deer on a sharp bend. Stuart got out of his vehicle and found the animal lying in front of the car lights motionless, but still alive. He went to the trunk of his car and took out his snow spade. He prepared with sorrow to deliver a merciful blow to take the poor unfortunate animal out of its agony. A mercy killing was required. He returned to the scene and stood at the front of the car, over the deer. He raised the spade above his head and summoned up the necessary force to dispatch the beast with hopefully no more than one fatal blow. On seeing the intent in his eyes and the spade above his shoulders, the young deer came to his senses and before anyone could say "Jack Robinson," it found its feet and darted at speed into the undergrowth nearby!

It just shows you that given a moments rest, our minds sometime return in time to take appropriate action.

I hope it is that way for you too. Good luck and remember you are never alone when you suffer a moment of memory loss.

Now, where are my spectacles?

Ah yes, I have just found them. I looked in a mirror and guess what? Yes, they were on my head!

Acknowledgements

The author is greatly indebted to general practitioner Dr. R. Sabur and nurse Helen Bryden, occupational health physician Dr. C. Jamieson, consultant psychiatrist Dr. D. Hall, and consultant clinical neuropsychologist Dr. J. Moore, all of Dumfries. They have brought me through my illness to a greater understanding of the mind and given me encouragement to live life to the fullest.

Professor Narinder Kapur, formerly at the Department of Neuropsychology, University of Southampton, and now at Addenbrookes Hospital, Cambridge, gave permission for me to quote extensively from his booklet "Managing Your Memory." Dr. Olwen Wilson, consultant psychologist and longtime friend, gave constructive criticism of the draft copy. My profound thanks go to both these distinguished psychologists.

Thanks to Alan, Margaret, Joyce, Stuart, Sean, Rachel, Jocelyn, Pamela, and Morag—the Kirkpatrick Durham badminton team. I leave them wondering whether my shots stem from the mind or the body. And special additional thanks go to Joyce for her graphic artwork on the cover of this book as well as her work on Operation Oboe and my other books.

A big hug across the Atlantic goes to Elizabeth Javor of Outskirts Press who has led me though the adaptation of this book into print in America. Thanks too to Derek Coates of Healthspan for permission to quote from the Healthspan booklet.

Finally, to Hans and Jutta in Germany, Peter and Elaine in Lancashire, Duke and Betty in Ghana and to Hannie and Joris in Belgium. To David and Jo in South Carolina, Hamish and Dahlia in Atlanta, Joan and Ian in London. To Tom and Abbey, John and Huerta, Bobby, Buck and Ziggy my four-legged friends. Because, like Mr. Dibdin…

"In every mess, I find a friend".
Charles Dibdin (1745-1814)

If you wish to contact the author or have a signed copy of this book or any other of his books sent to you or a friend, please provide your information through the following e-mail address, or send it to me at: Netherholm, Edinburgh Road, Dumfries, DG1 1JX Scotland.

Mhcaldwell@btopenworld.com

Meanwhile, you are most welcome to visit:
www.millercaldwell.org

and even more writing, poetry and pictures of Ghana, the UK and Pakistan at AuthorsDen.com/miller caldwell

LaVergne, TN USA
12 November 2009
163941LV00002B/65/P